2399053 3

The Life and Work of... Paul Klee

Sean Connolly

Heinemann Library
Des Plaines, Illinois

© 2000 Reed Educational & Professional Publishing
Published by Heinemann Library,
an imprint of Reed Educational & Professional Publishing,
1350 East Touhy Avenue, Suite 240 West
Des Plaines, IL 60018

Customer Service 1-888-454-2279

Designed by Celia Floyd
Illustrations by Kim Harley
Printed in Hong Kong, China

04 03 02 01 00
10 9 8 7 6 5 4 3 2 1

Library of Congress Cataloging-in-Publication Data
Connolly, Sean, 1956-
    Paul Klee / Sean Connolly.
        p. cm. – (The life and work of--) (Heinemann profiles)
    Includes bibliographical references and index.
        Summary: Introduces the life and work of Paul Klee, discussing his early years, life in Switzerland and Germany, and development as an artist.
        ISBN 1-57572-952-0 (Lib. binding)
        1. Klee, Paul, 1879-1940 Juvenile literature. 2. Artists—Germany Biography Juvenile literature. [1. Klee, Paul, 1879-1940.
    2. Artists. 3. Painting, German. 4. Art appreciation.] I. Title.
    II. Series. III. Series: Heinemann profiles.
    N6888.K55C665 1999
    760'.092—dc21
    [B]   99-14548
                                                           CIP

Acknowledgments

The Publishers would like to thank the following for permission to reproduce photographs:

AKG Photo, pp. 4, 10, 22, 24 Paul-Klee-Stiftung, Kunstmuseum, Bern/L Moillet, p.20. Fotopress/Walter Henggeler, p. 28; Page 5, Paul Klee, *Familienspaziergang*, 1930, 264, Credit: Paul-Klee-Stiftung, Kunstmuseum, Bern. Page 7, Paul Klee, *Dünen landschaft*, 19213, 139, Credit: Paul-Klee-Stiftung, Kunstmuseum, Bern. Page 9, Paul Klee, *Schadau*, 1895/96, Credit: Paul-Klee-Stiftung, Kunstmuseum, Bern. Page 11, Paul Klee, *Siebzehn, irr.* 1923, Credit: Oeffentliche Kunstsammlung Kupferstichkabinett, Basel. Page 13, Paul Klee, *Meine Bude*, 1896, Credit: Paul-Klee-Stiftung, Kunstmuseum, Bern. Page 15, Paul Klee, *Lily*, 1905, 32, Credit: Paul-Klee-Stiftung, Kunstmuseum, Bern. Page 17, Paul Klee, *Candide 7. Capitel "Il lève le voile d'une main timide,"* 1911, 63, Credit: Paul-Klee-Stiftung, Kunstmuseum, Bern. Page 19, Paul Klee, Mädchen mit Krügen, Credit: Paul-Klee-Stiftung, Kunstmuseum, Bern. Page 21, Paul Klee, *Rote und Weisse Kuppeln*, 1914, 45, Credit: AKG Photo. Page 23, Paul Klee, *Einst dem Grau der Nacht enttaucht…*, 1918, 17, Credit: Paul-Klee-Stiftung, Kunstmuseum, Bern. Page 25, Paul Klee, *Plan einer garten-architektur*, 1920, 214, Credit: Bridgeman Art Library. Page 27, Paul Klee *Polyphon gefasstes Weiss*, 1930, 140(x10), Credit: Paul-Klee-Stiftung, Kunstmuseum, Bern. Page 29, Paul Klee, *TOD und FEUER*, 1940, 332 (G 12), Credit: Paul-Klee-Stiftung, Kunstmuseum, Bern.

Cover photograph reproduced with permission of Bridgeman Art Library

Our thanks to Paul Flux for his comments in the preparation of this book.

Every effort has been made to contact copyright holders of any material reproduced in this book. Any omissions will be rectified in subsequent printings if notice is given to the Publisher.

Some words in this book are in bold, **like this.** You can find out what they mean by looking in the glossary.

Contents

Who Was Paul Klee?   4

Early Years   6

School Days   8

The Move to Germany   10

Learning to Paint   12

A Growing Family   14

Public Success   16

A Friendly Welcome   18

Color Takes Hold   20

New Directions   22

Time as a Teacher   24

Escape from Germany   26

Illness and Death   28

Timeline   30

Glossary   *31*

Index   *32*

More Books to Read   *32*

More Artwork to See   *32*

Who Was Paul Klee?

Paul Klee was a Swiss painter and a **graphic artist**. He liked to make very colorful paintings. His pictures make people think of music and dreams.

Paul kept a sense of fun in his paintings. This picture shows how he liked to "take a line for a walk."

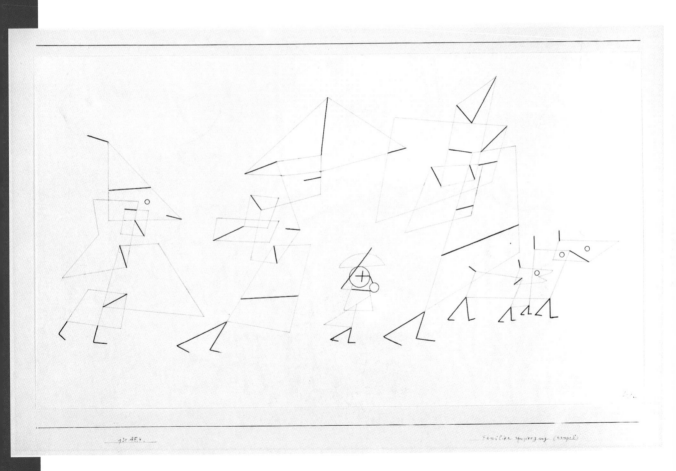

Early Years

Paul Klee was born on December 18, 1879. He was born near Berne, Switzerland. His family loved music. Paul learned to play the violin when he was seven years old.

Paul's uncle Ernst had a café. Paul liked to look at the patterns on the tablecloths. This painting was made in 1923. It shows that Paul was still interested in patterns.

1923 139 Dünen landschaft

School Days

Paul went to school in Berne, Switzerland. He still enjoyed music. He joined the Berne **Orchestra** when he was only 10 years old.

Paul also liked to draw pictures. He filled his school notebooks with drawings and designs. He tried to show his love of music and poetry in his paintings.

The Move to Germany

Paul left school when he was 19 years old. He moved to Munich, Germany. He began to **study** drawing and painting. Magazines like this helped him to think of funny ideas.

Paul had a good sense of humor. He made this picture in 1923. He was 44 years old. It shows his sense of humor in his work.

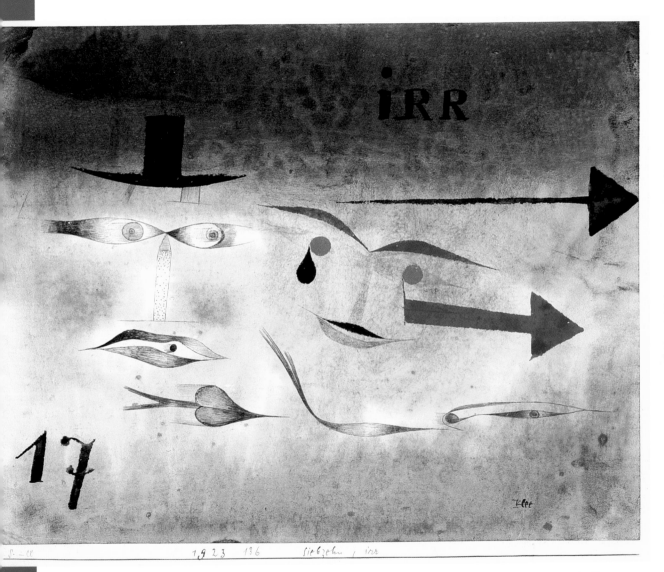

Learning to Paint

Paul **studied** paintings in Italy when he was 22 years old. He then returned to his family in Switzerland. He **practiced** his own art. He tried many different ideas.

Most of Paul's works were drawings or **etchings**.
This drawing of his bedroom shows how well Paul
could draw.

A Growing Family

In 1906, Paul married Lily Stumpf. Their son Felix was born one year later. Lily earned money by playing piano **concerts**. Paul worked at home.

Some of Paul's **etchings** were **exhibited** in Munich in 1906. Paul became better known after the exhibit. This is a painting of Lily.

Public Success

Paul's first one-man **exhibit** was in Berne in 1910. It was a great success. The same exhibit was shown in other cities in Switzerland.

Paul's pictures were black and white. He used an ink pen and drew on white paper. This picture was used in a book.

A Friendly Welcome

Paul became friends with August Macke and Wassily Kandinsky. In 1911, Paul joined their group of **expressionist** artists. The group was called Der Blaue Reiter (The Blue Rider).

Paul also liked the work of other artists. He painted this picture in 1910. It looks like a painting by an artist named Paul Cézanne.

Color Takes Hold

In 1914, Paul and August Macke visited Tunisia, a country in Africa. Paul loved the bright light and colors he saw there. He decided to stop using just black and white in his pictures.

Lote u. weisse Kuppeln 1914.45

This painting shows how Paul began to use colors.
The colored squares look like the **mosaics** he saw
in Tunisia.

New Directions

Paul liked painting with many colors. He felt free to try other new ideas, too. He started putting letters and numbers in his pictures.

Paul thought numbers and letters made people think of words and dreams. Paul felt he was making a new **language** in his pictures.

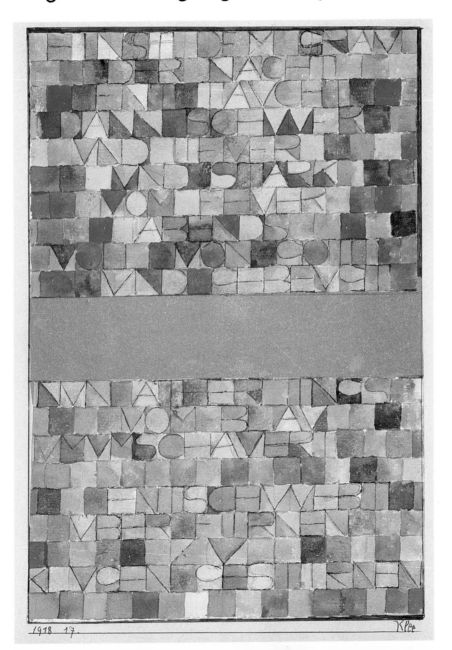

Time as a Teacher

In 1920, Paul became a teacher at the Bauhaus. The Bauhaus was the most famous art school in Germany. Paul taught there until 1931.

Paul's pictures show what he taught at the
Bauhaus. He taught students that an artist is like
a tree trunk. The tree branches are the thoughts
an artist shows in the artwork.

25

Escape from Germany

A new **government**, called the **Nazis**, took power in Germany. They did not like Paul's pictures or those of many other artists. Paul had to move to Switzerland in 1933.

The Nazis wanted pictures to look like real things. Paul did not agree. He wanted his colors and lines to make people think for themselves.

Illness and Death

When Paul was 56 years old, he became very ill. He still painted, but he was in constant pain. Paul's illness made him think about death and war.

His pictures became darker. Thick black lines replaced the bright colors he used when he was well. Paul died in Muralto, Switzerland, on June 29, 1940. He was 61 years old.

Timeline

1879	Paul Klee born, December 18
1886	Paul begins to **study** the violin.
1889	Paul joins Berne Municipal **Orchestra**
1893	First motion picture camera developed in France
1898	Paul leaves school and moves to Munich, Germany
1903	The Wright brothers fly the first airplane
1906	Paul marries Lily Stumpf and has **etchings exhibited**
1910	Paul has successful exhibits in Switzerland
1911	Paul joins group of **expressionist** artists
1914	Paul visits Tunisia and decides to fill his pictures with color
1914–18	**World War I**
1920–31	Paul teaches at the Bauhaus art school in Germany
1927	Charles Lindbergh makes first solo flight across the Atlantic
1933	Paul forced to leave Germany and go to Switzerland
1935	Paul begins long illness
1939	**World War II** begins in Europe
1940	Paul dies, June 29

Glossary

concert   music played in public

etching   picture made by drawing on a metal plate and then printing it

exhibit   to show and sell works of art in public

expressionist   artist who tries to show feelings about things in paintings

government   group of people who rule a country

graphic artist   someone who makes pictures to print

language   something a person uses to let others know what they think or feel

mosaics   pattern of colored stone used to make a picture

Nazi   short name for the National Socialist German Workers' Party

orchestra   group of musicians that plays concerts in public

practice   to do something again and again to be able to do it better

study   learn about a subject

World War I   war in Europe that lasted from 1914–1918

World War II   war that was fought in Europe, Africa, and Asia from 1939–1945

Index

Africa   20, 21
Bauhaus   24, 25
Berne   6, 8, 12, 16
born   6
Der Blaue Reiter (The Blue Rider)
    18
died   28
drawings
    Candide 7. Capitel "He raises the veil
        with a timid hand" 1911, 63   17
    My Room, 1896   13
Ernst (uncle)   7
Italy   12
Kandinsky, Wassily   18
Klee, Felix   14
Macke, August   18, 20
Munich   10, 15
Nazis   26, 27

paintings
    A Family Walk   5
    DEATH and FIRE, 1949, 332 (G 12)
        29
    Dunes Landscape, 19213, 139   7
    Girl with Pitchers   19
    Lily, 1905, 32   15
    Once upon a time, emerging out
        of the gray of the night...   23
    Plan of a Garden Architecture,
        1920, 214   25
    Polyphonically Framed White
        1930, 140 (x10)   27
    Red and White Domes 1914, 45   21
    Schadau, 1895/96   9
    Seventeen, irr. 1923   11
Stumpf, Lily   14

More Books to Read

Raboff, Ernest. *Paul Klee.* New York: HarperCollins Children's Books, 1988.

Venezia, Mike. *Paul Klee.* Danbury, Conn.: Children's Press, 1991.

An older reader can help you with these books.

More Artwork to See

New House in the Suburbs, 1924. National Gallery of Art, Washington, D.C.

Land of Lemons, 1929. The Philips Collection, Washington, D.C.

Trees Behind Rocks, 1929. The Solomon R. Guggenheim Museum, New York.